Esse & Friends

Handwriting
Practice Workbook
alphabet

Size 2 | US | Travel

Esse & Friends Learning Books

Esse & Friends Handwriting Practice WorkBook: Alphabet

(c) 2019 Esse & Friends Learning Books. All rights reserved.

ISBN: 978-0-6487389-8-8

This book:
- Paperback
- Travel size
- Practice Lines: Size 2 (1.5 cm)

Series: Esse & Friends Learning Workbook: Alphabet

Esse & Friends Learning Workbooks:
- Esse's Friends
- Alphabet
- Numbers
- Shapes
- Colours (UK)
- Colors (US)

The Esse & Friends Learning books aim to help preschool, kindergarten and primary school aged children to have fun coloring in and practicing their handwriting skills while enjoying the Esse & Friends characters.

This book belongs to:

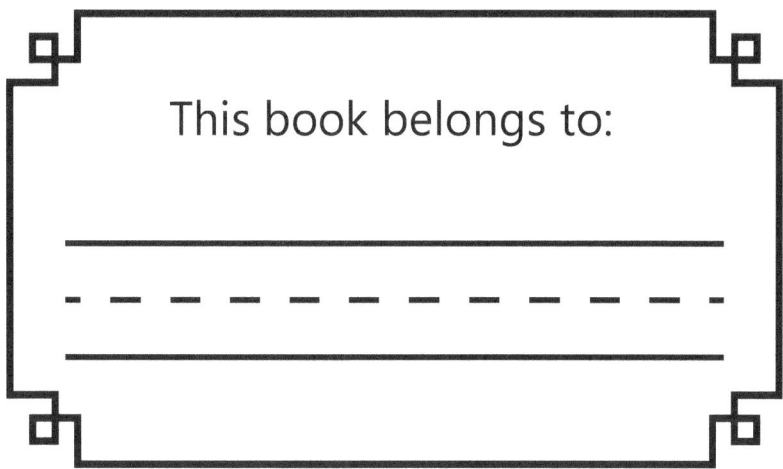

Color me in!

Esse & Friends Learning Books

B B B B B B B B

B B B B B B B B

B B B B B B B B B B

B B B B B B B B B B

F F F F F F F F F F

F F F F F F F F F F

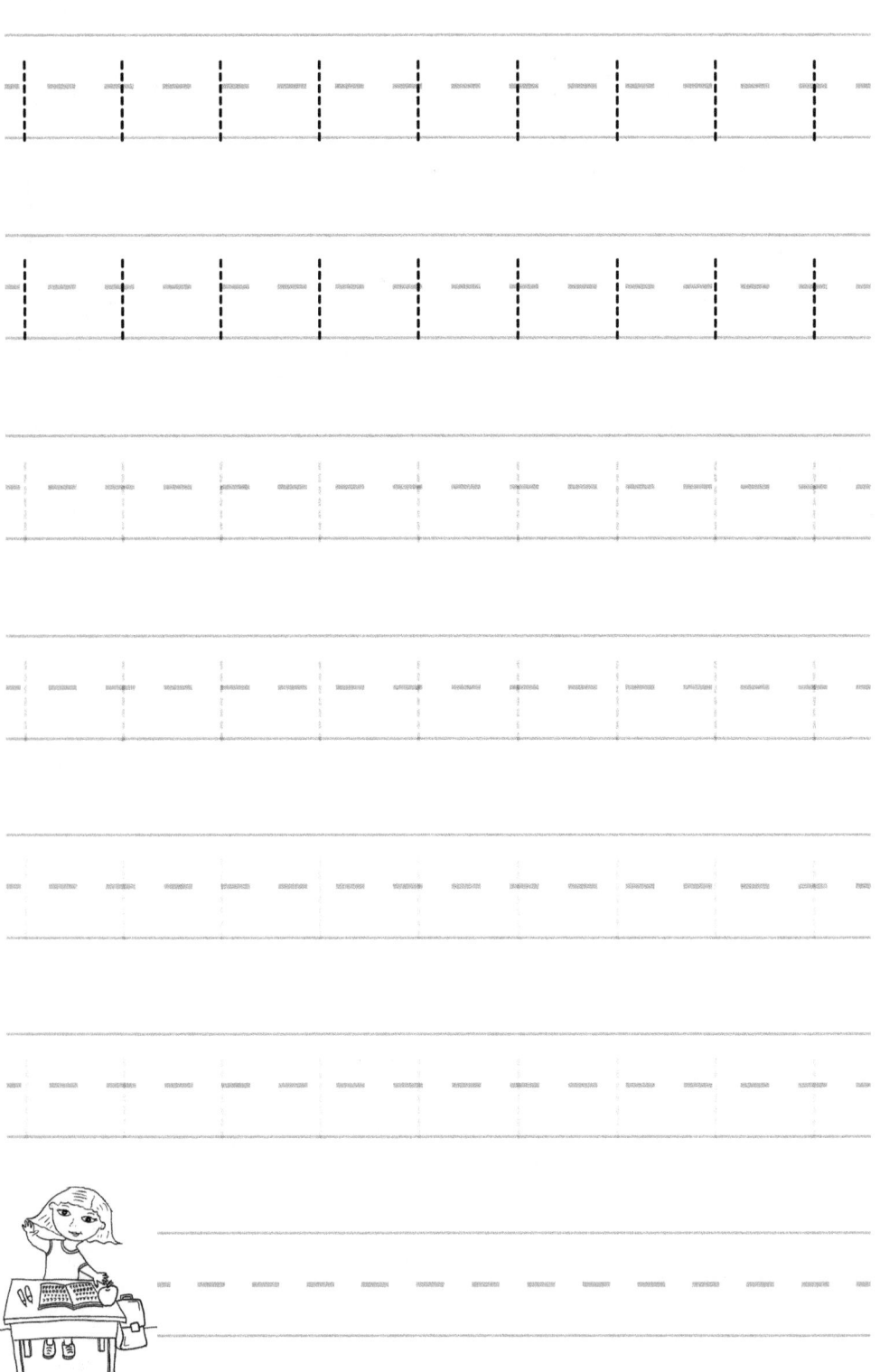

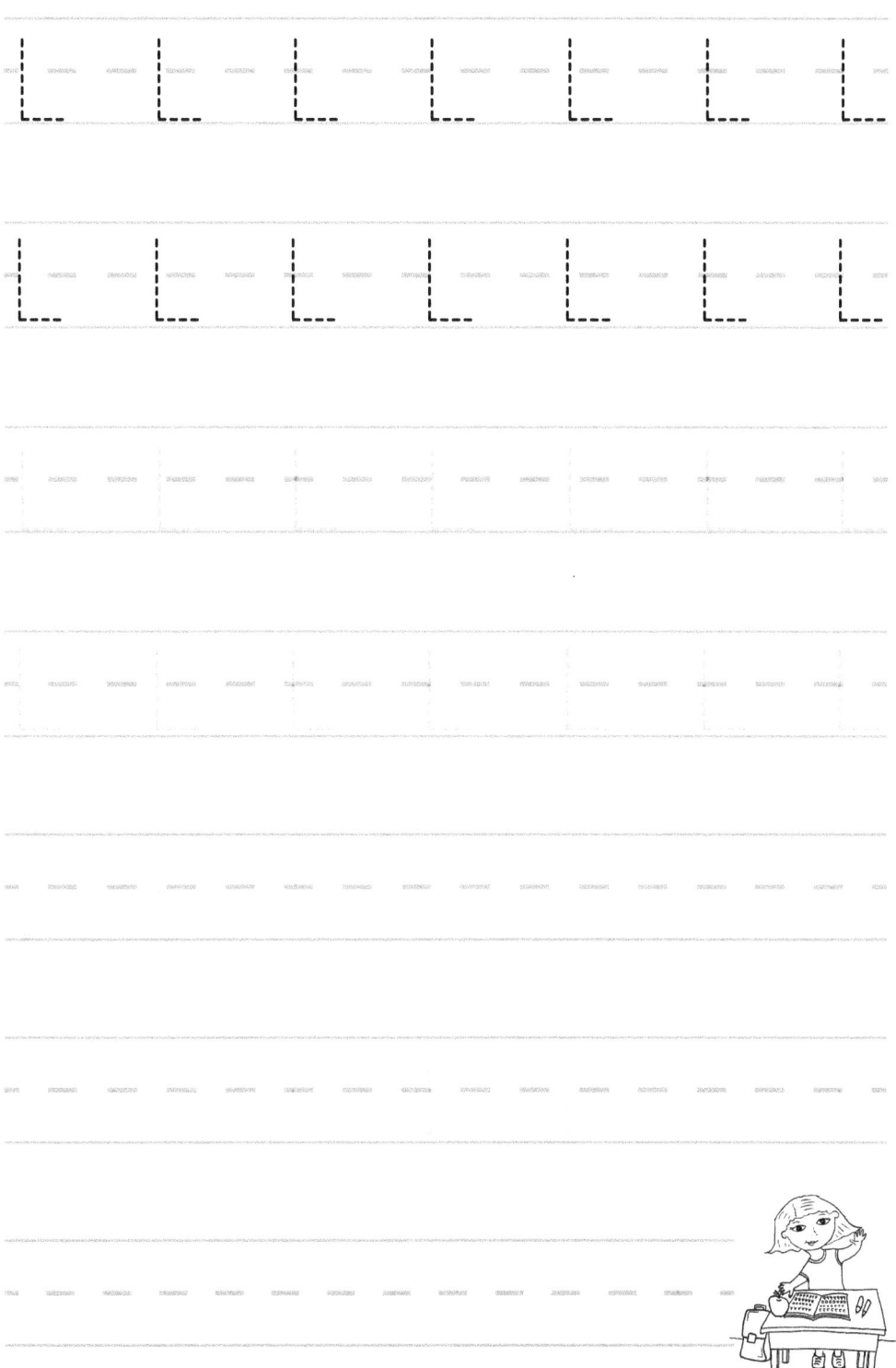

p p p p p p

p p p p p p

p p p p p p

p p p p p p

p p p p p p

p p p p p p

R   R   R   R   R   R   R

R   R   R   R   R   R   R

R   R   R   R   R   R   R

R   R   R   R   R   R   R

T T T T T T

T T T T T T

y y y y y y y

y y y y y y y

Esse & Friends
Learning Books

Attention Parents and Educators!
You are welcome to contact us to enquire about our bulk purchasing discounts and discuss our creating custom words and Esse & Friends interiors.

Be sure to check out the other Coloring and Handwriting Practice Workbooks in this series. Just look for Esse on the cover!

www.ingramcontent.com/pod-product-compliance
Lightning Source LLC
Chambersburg PA
CBHW072101290426
44110CB00014B/1776